Doodle to Intent: Inner Chaos
Book 3, Doodle to Intent series.
Published by NoooBooks, 2020
Tweed Heads, NSW, Australia.
Copyright: © NoooBooks

Dude LI. © 2020 All rights reserved.

Without limiting the rights under copyright reserved above, no part of this
publication may be reproduced, stored in or introduced into a retrieval system, or
transmitted, in any form or by any means
(electronic, mechanical, photocopying, recording or otherwise)
without the prior written permission of the publishers of this book.

Traditional pen & ink and brush & ink illustrations.

The paper this book is printed on is FSC® certified (Forest Stewardship Council®).
FSC promotes environmentally responsible, socially beneficial and
economically viable management of the world's forests.

A catalogue record for this book is available
from the National Library of Australia.
Hardback ISBN: 978-1-922415-05-9
Paperback ISBN: 978-1-922415-06-6

# Doodle to INTENT

### INNER CHAOS

by Dude Ll.

"What if your looks changed completely?

Every time you had a different mood—

—Or a new thought?"

How would we know who we are?

Would my loved ones still recognise me?

A bit plain?

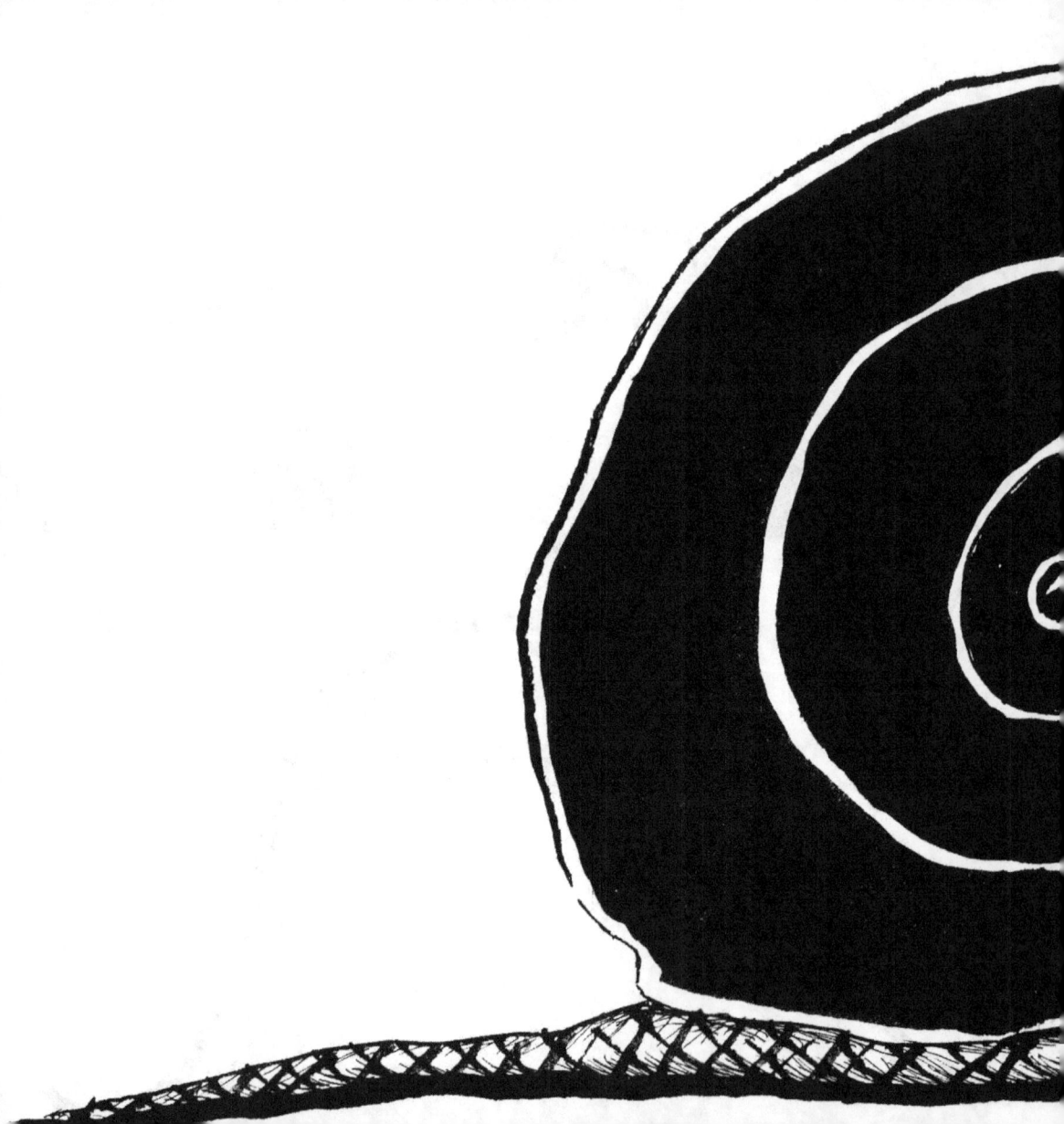

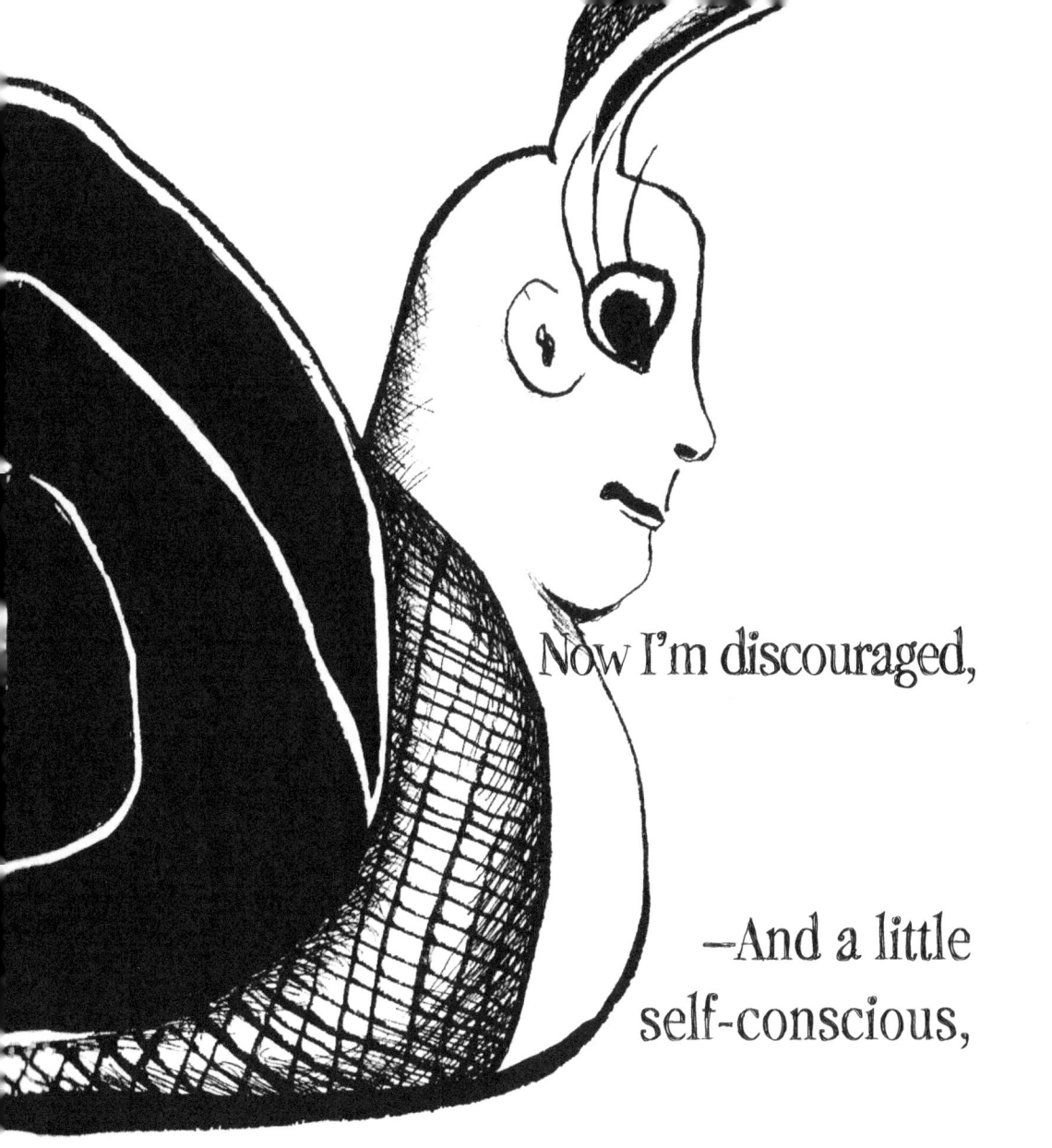

A little dazed,

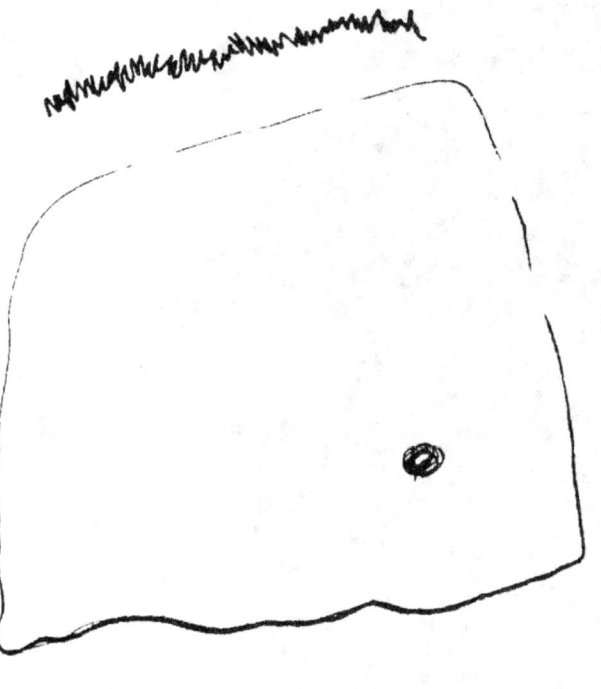

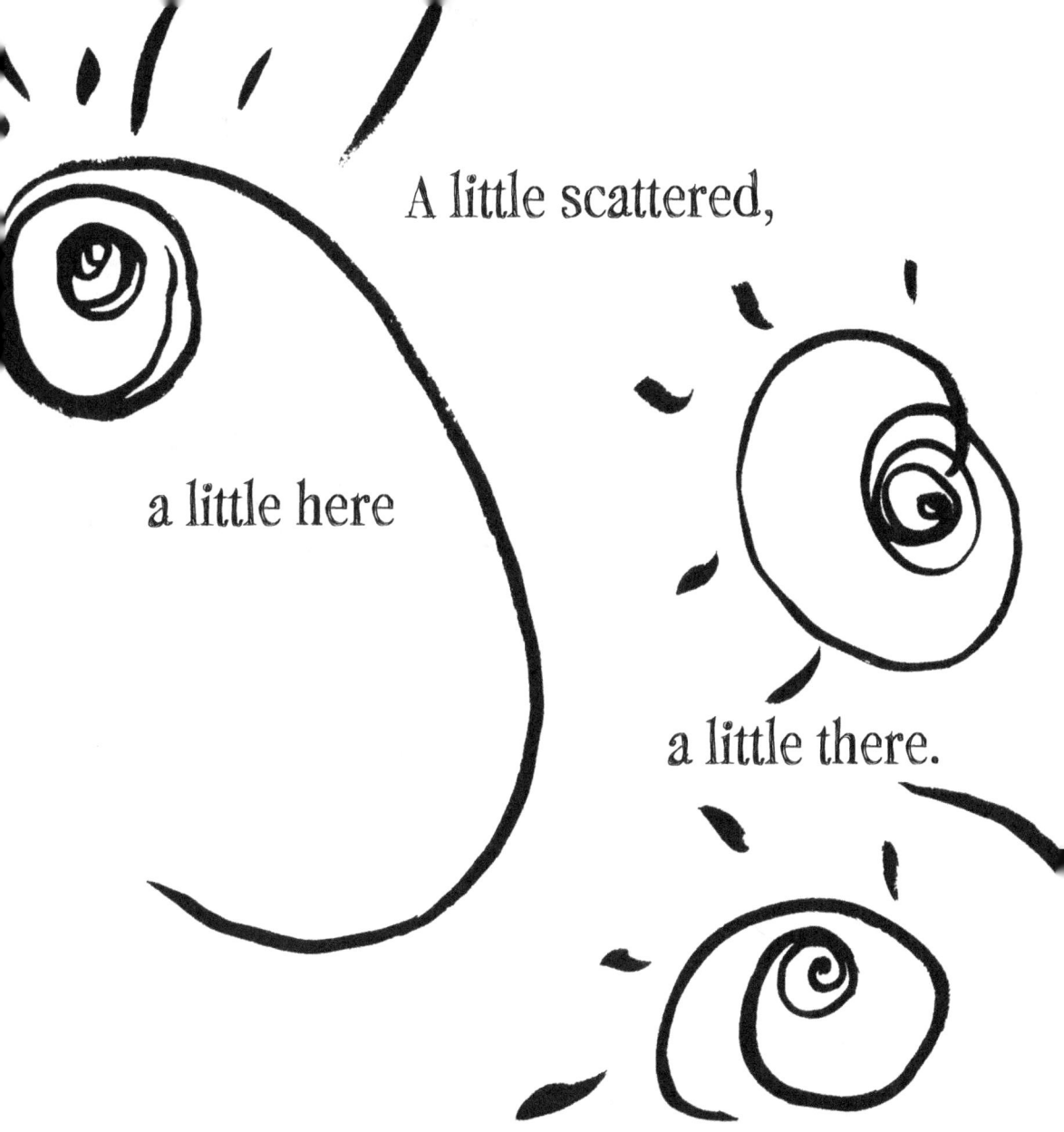

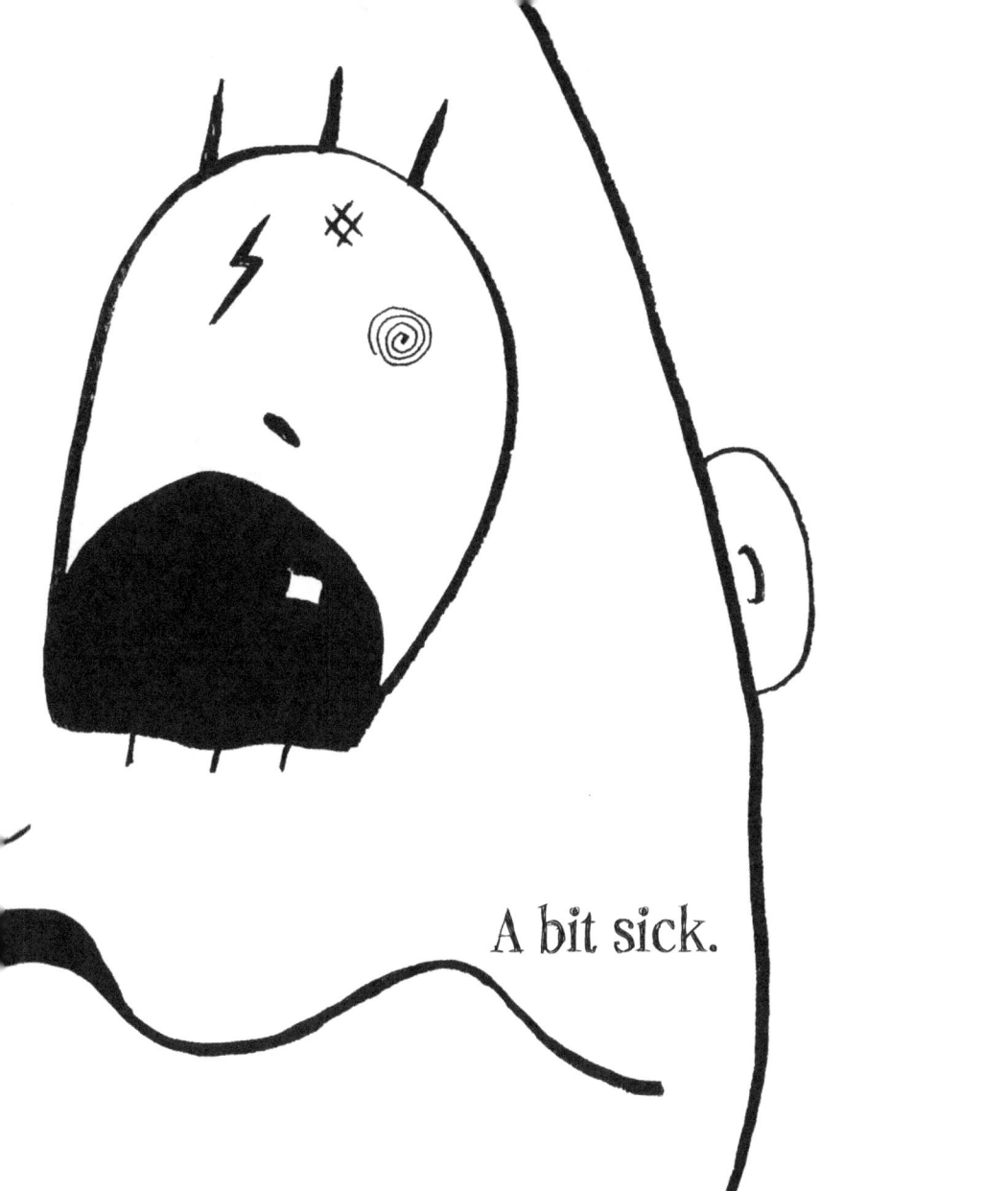

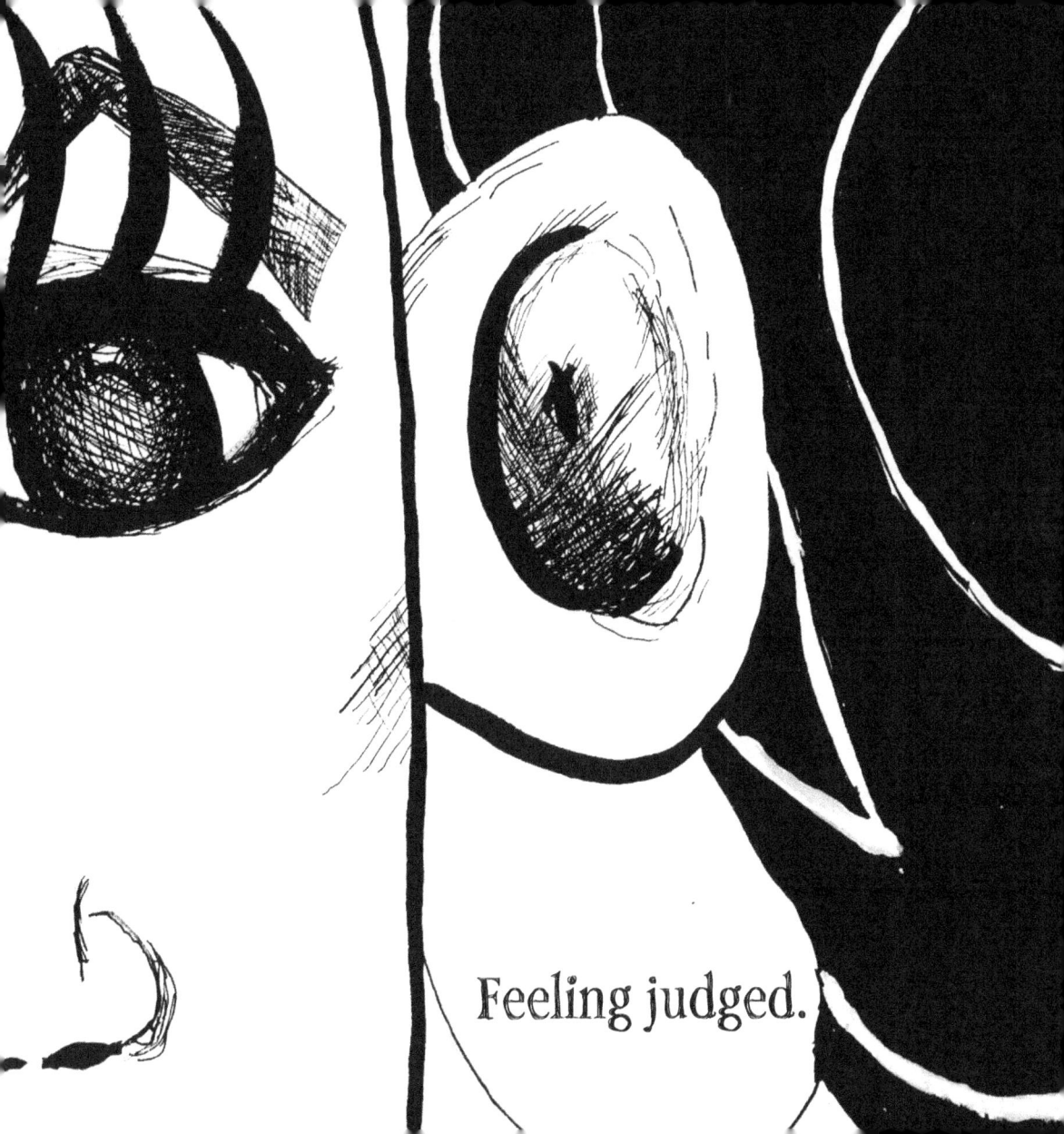

My thoughts start racing...

Right,
Wrong,
   Purity,
     Good,
Have to,
  Should,
  Need,
        Do,
  Don't,
     Will,
      Can,
Can't,
   Did,
     Won't
Shan't.

Feeling bitter,

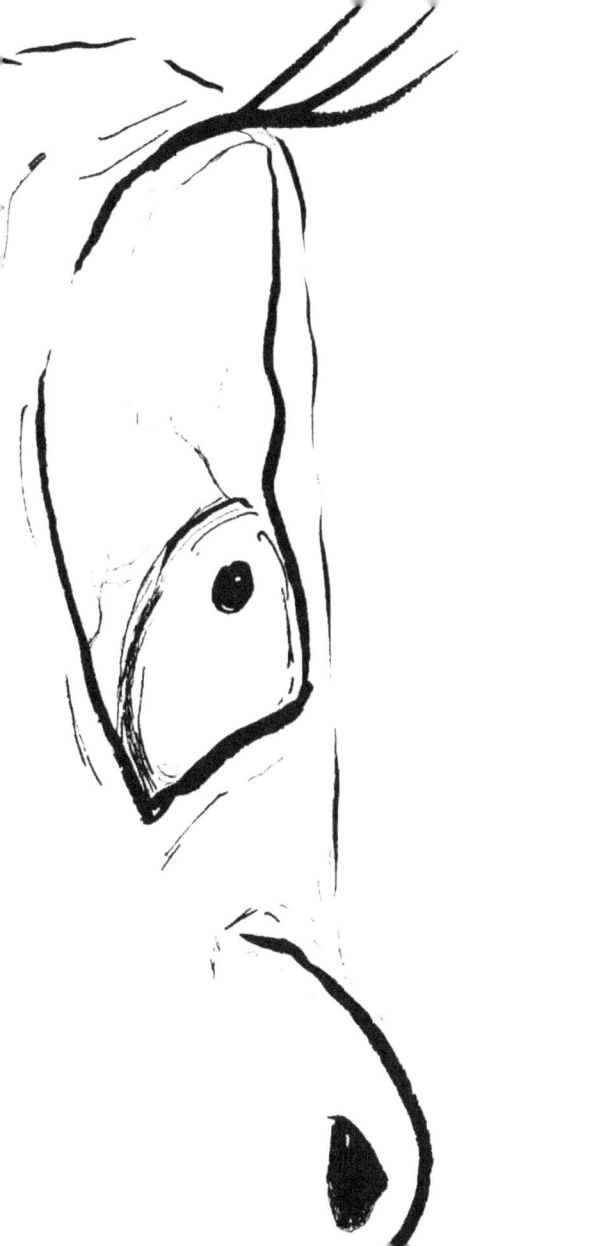

And a bit angry,

And confused.

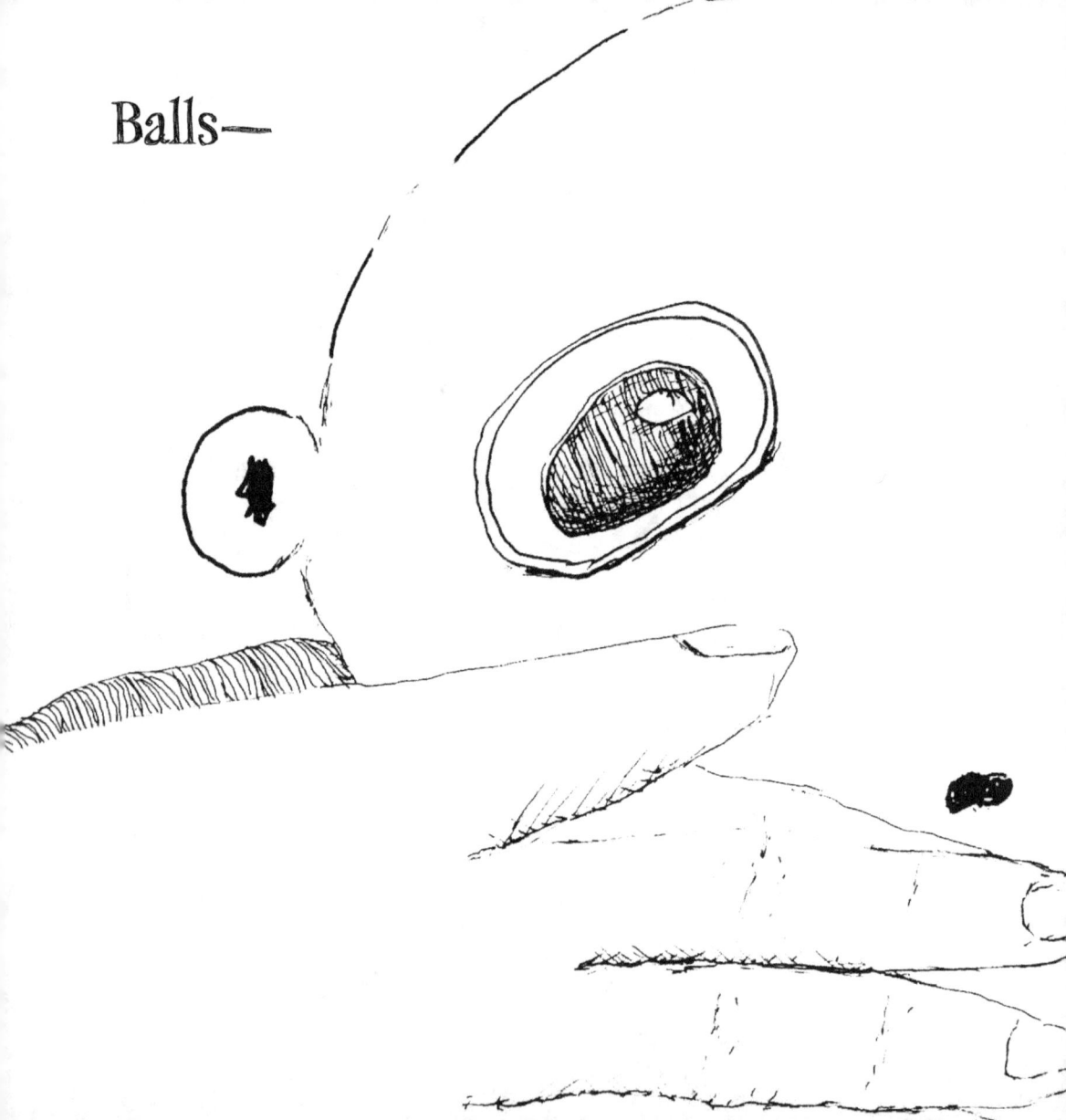

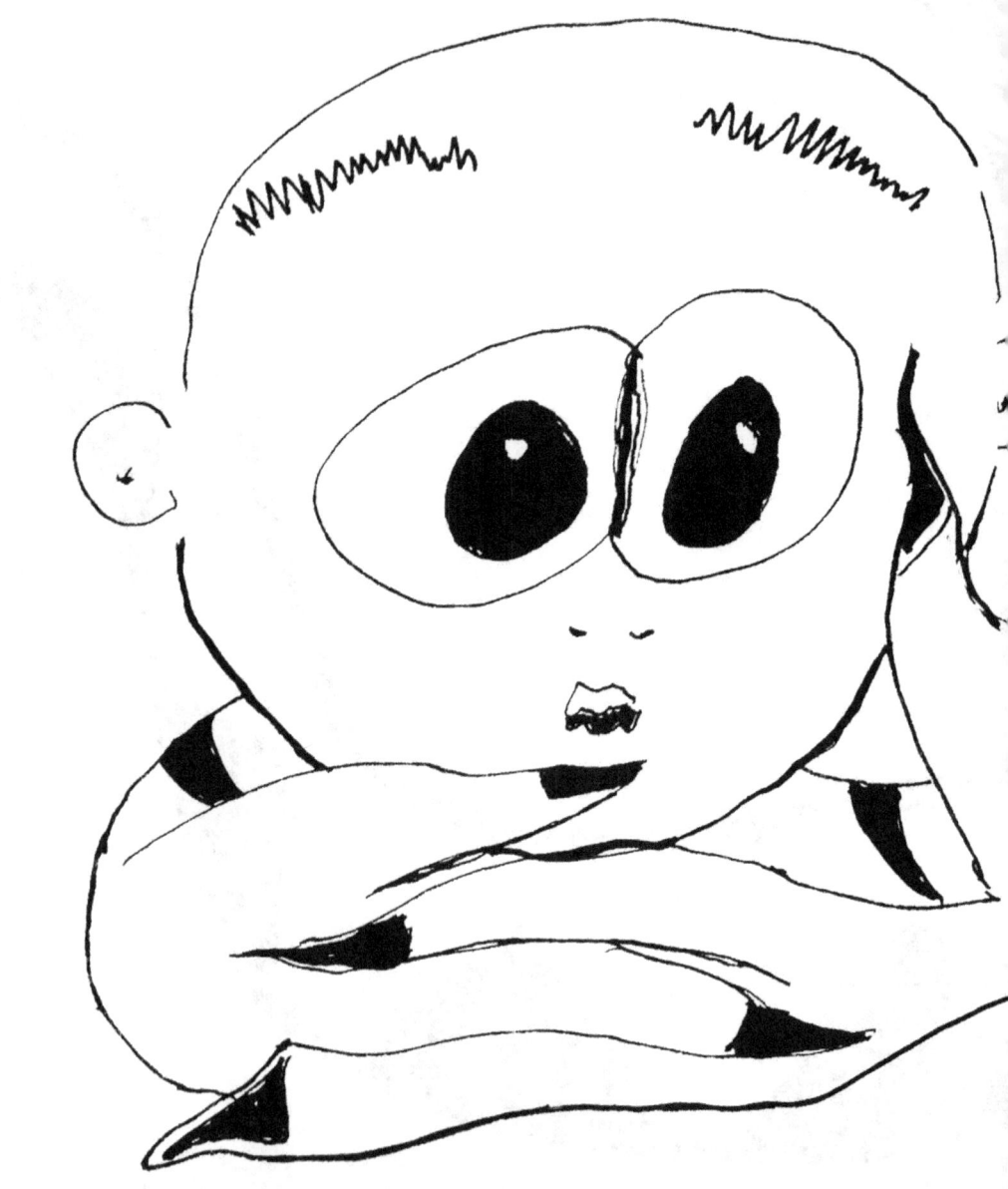

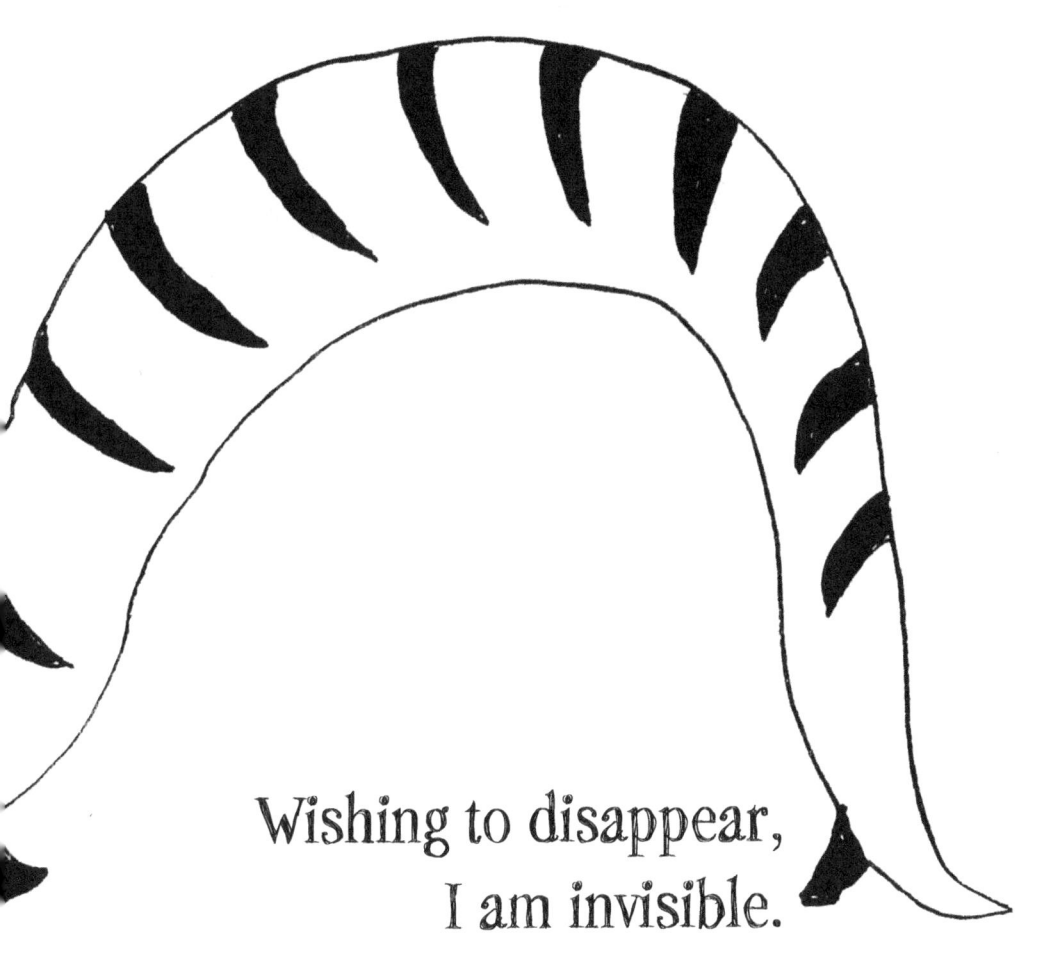

Wishing to disappear,
I am invisible.

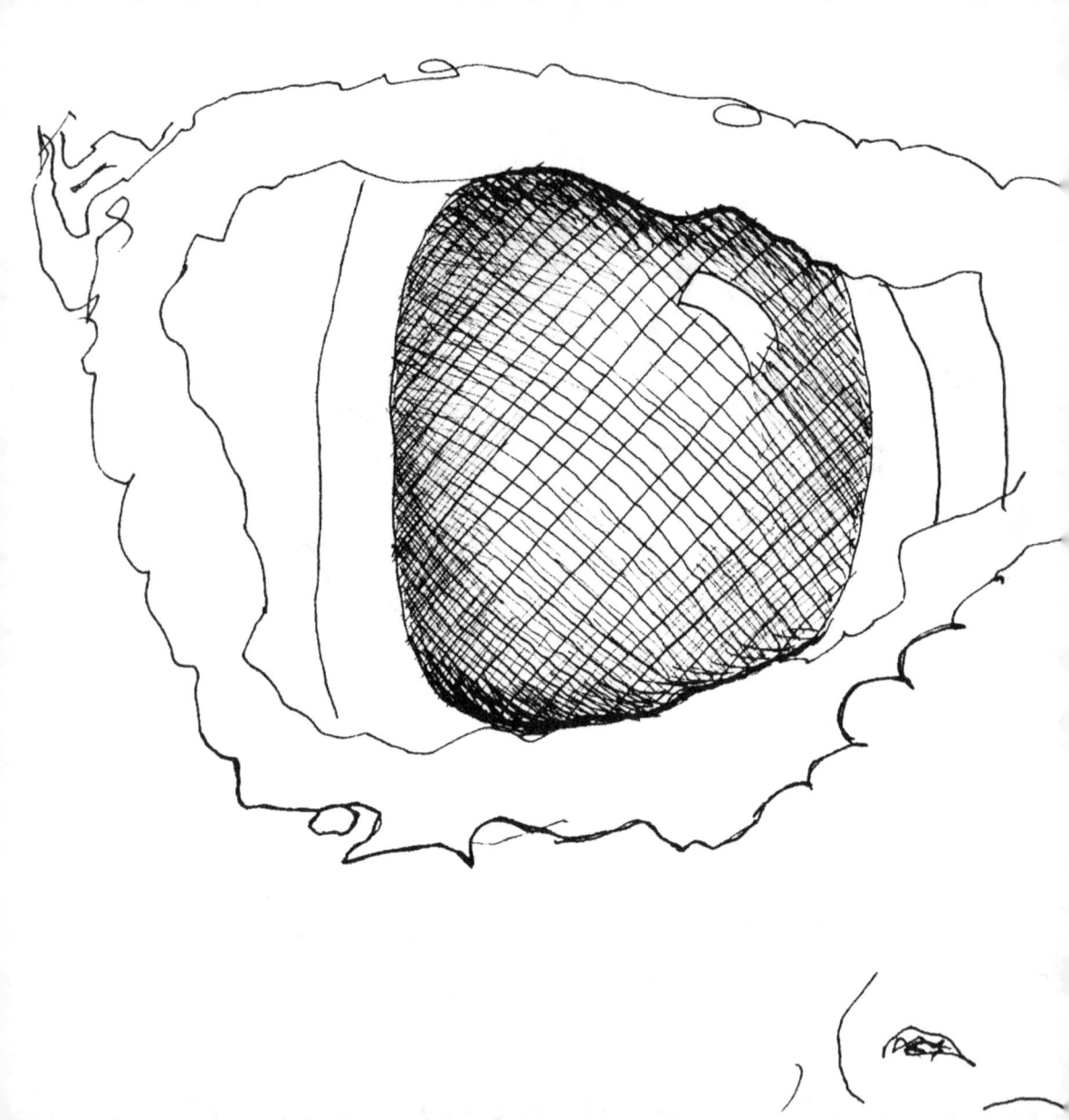

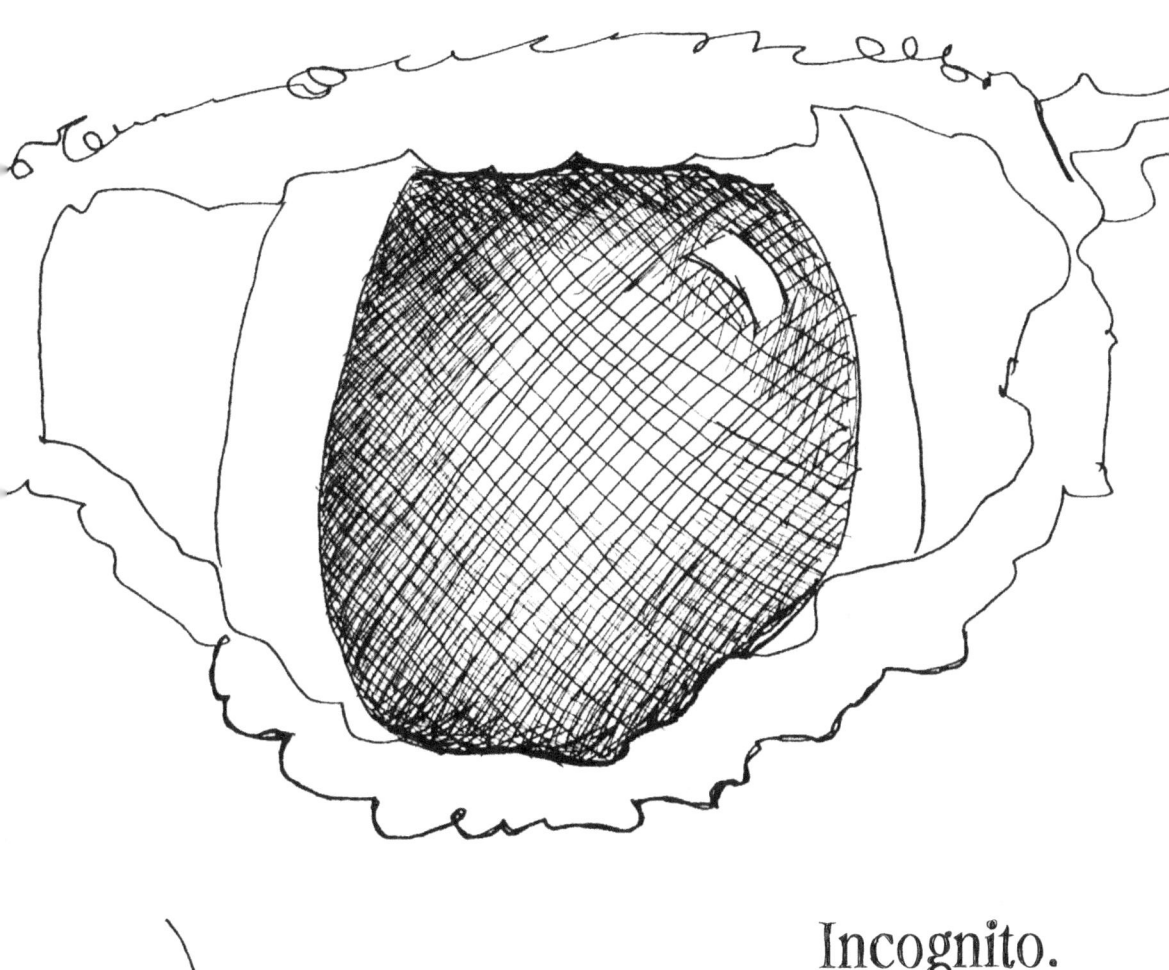

Incognito.

Leave the confusion behind.

Time to zen,

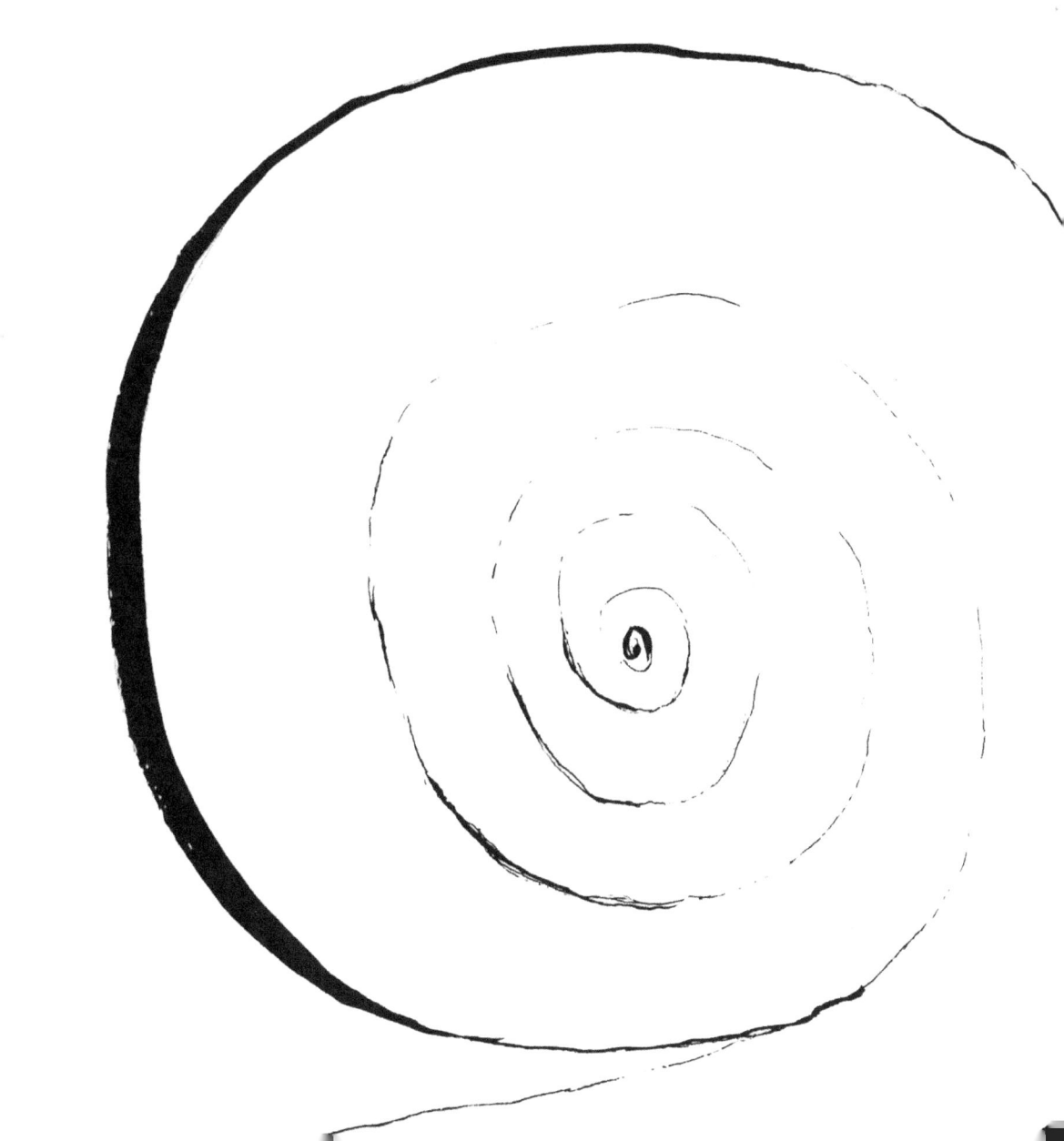

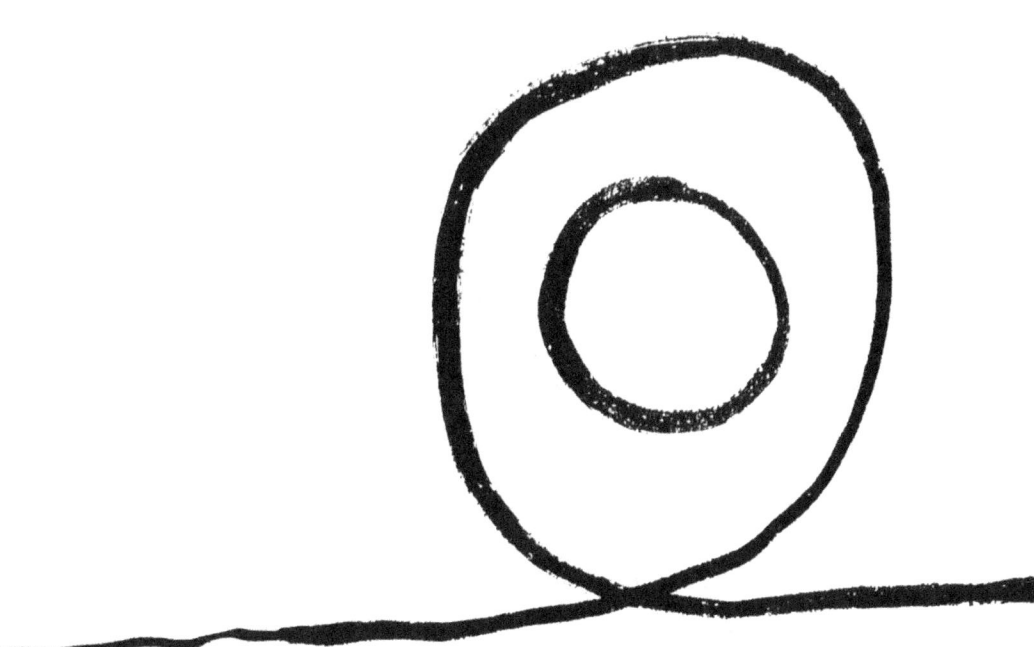

Rediscover my roots,

Feel who I am, just be me,

Everything,

is A-OK

Be content.

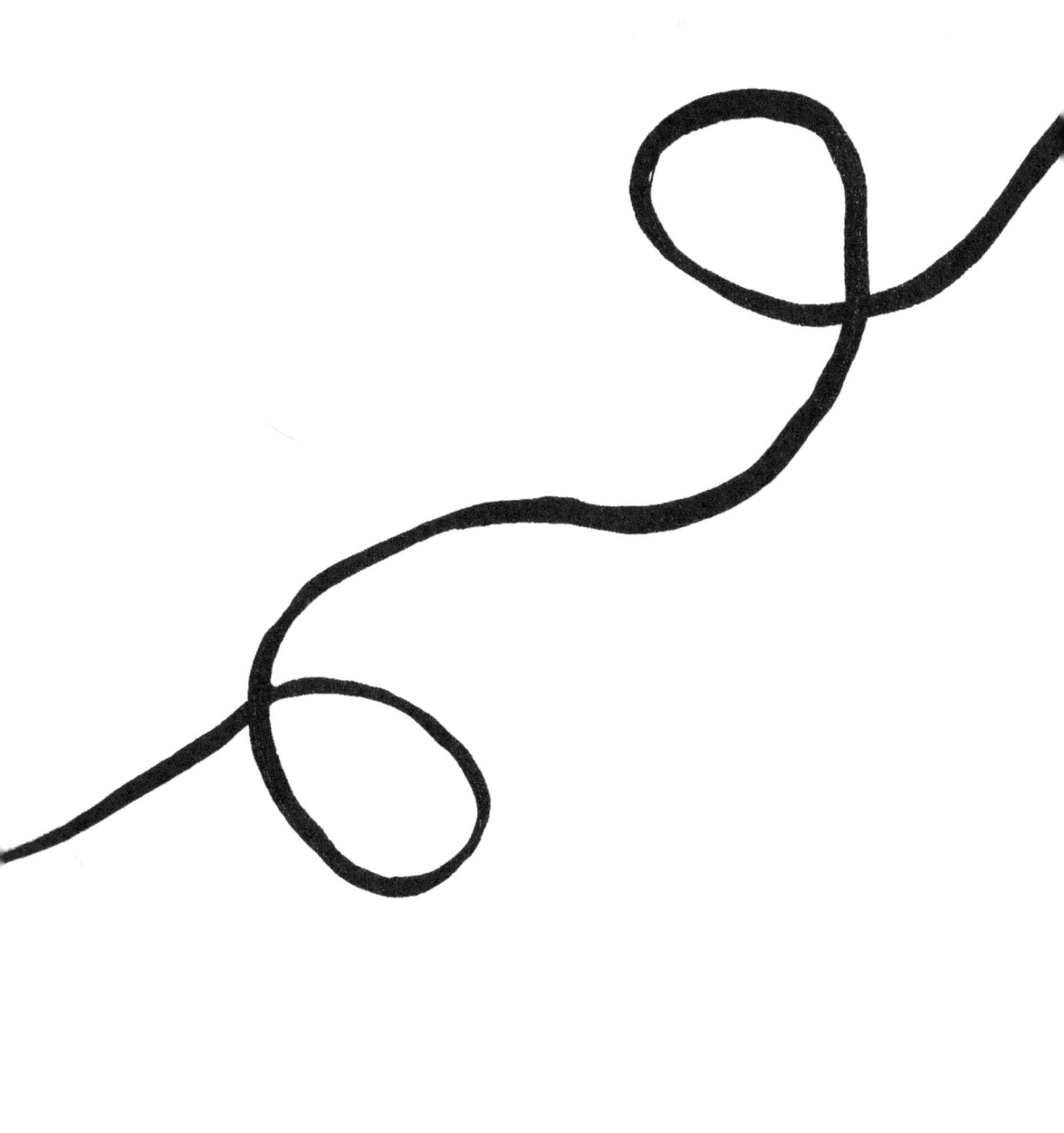

–A little bit of doubt...

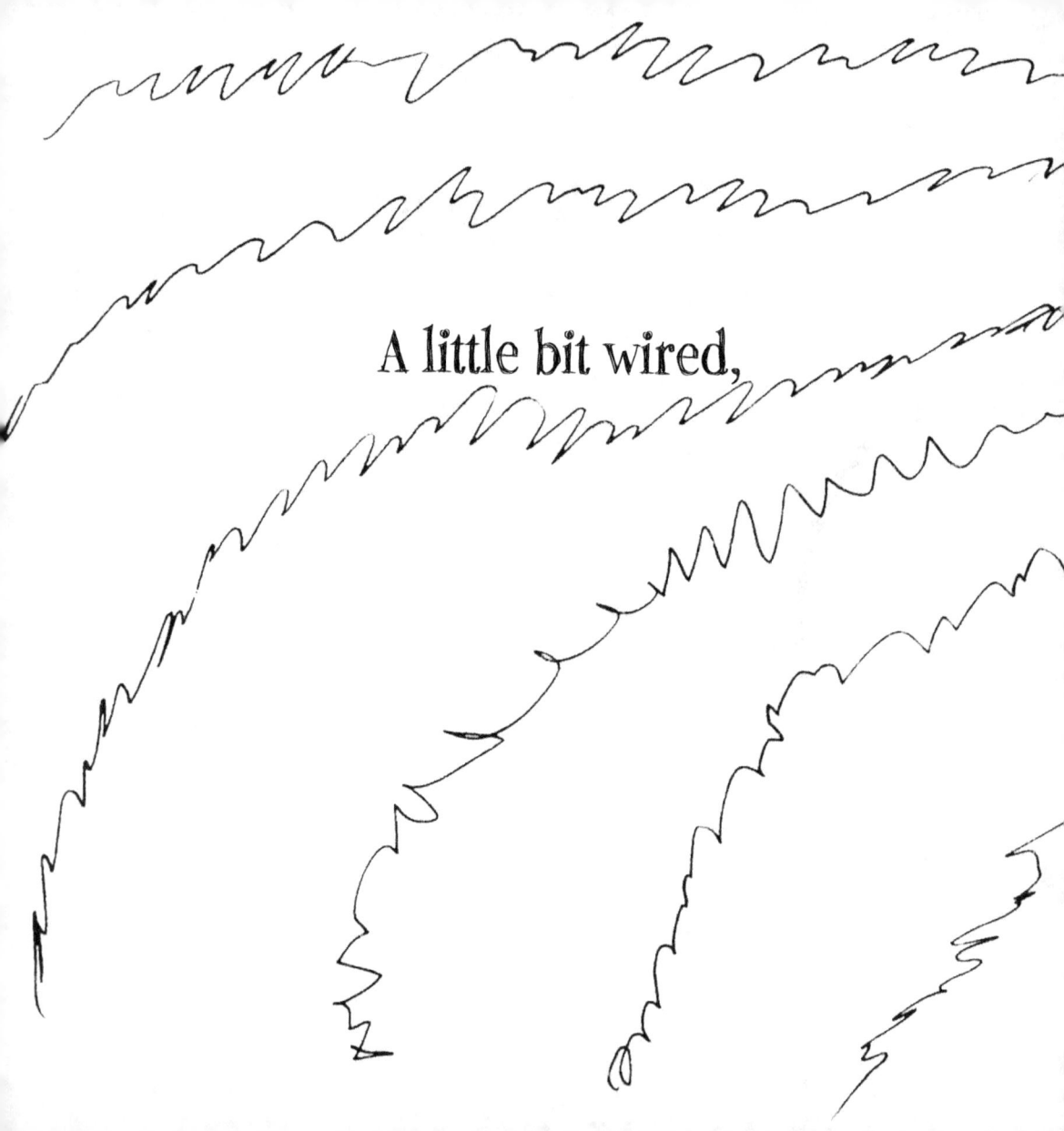
A little bit wired,

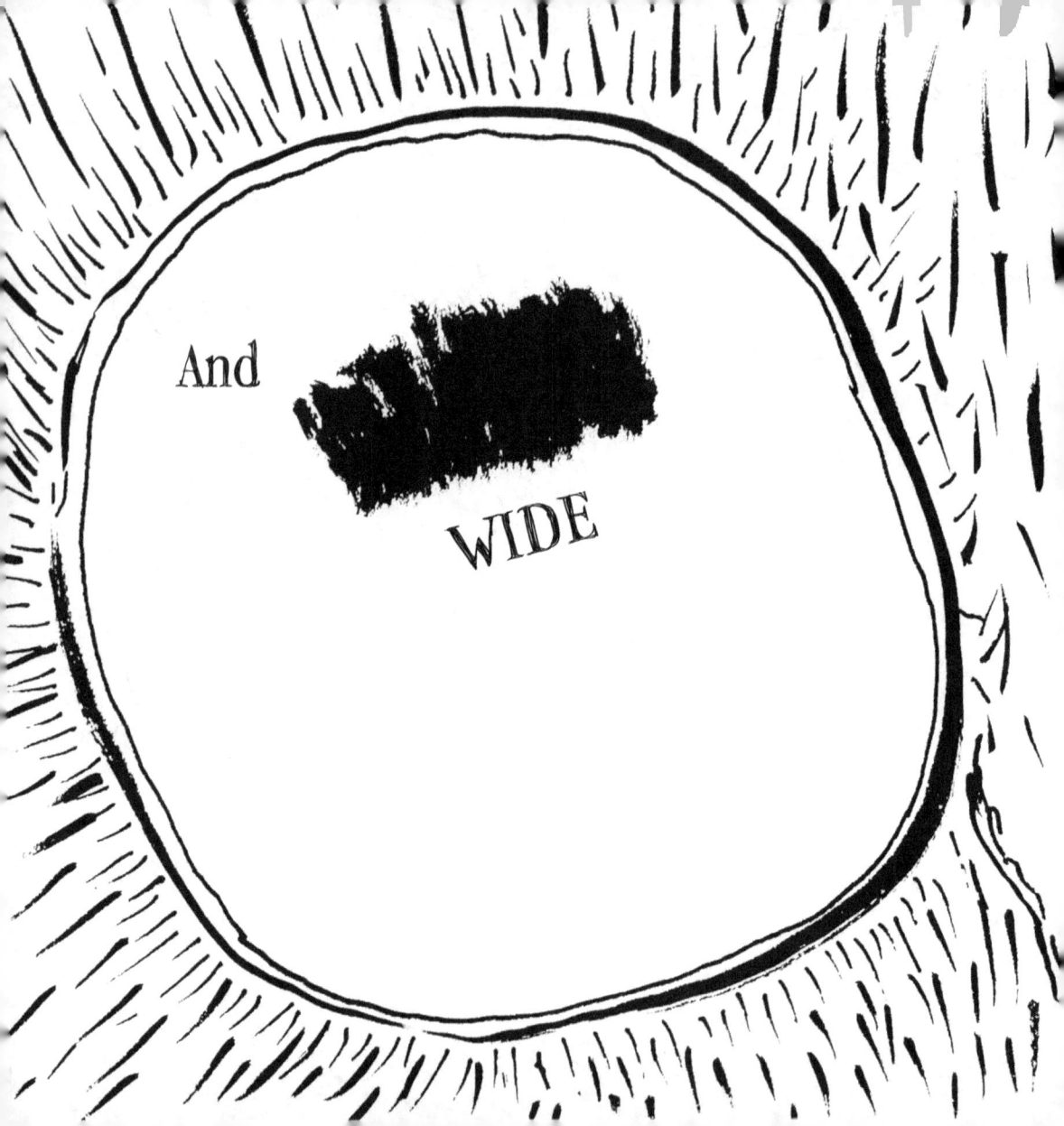

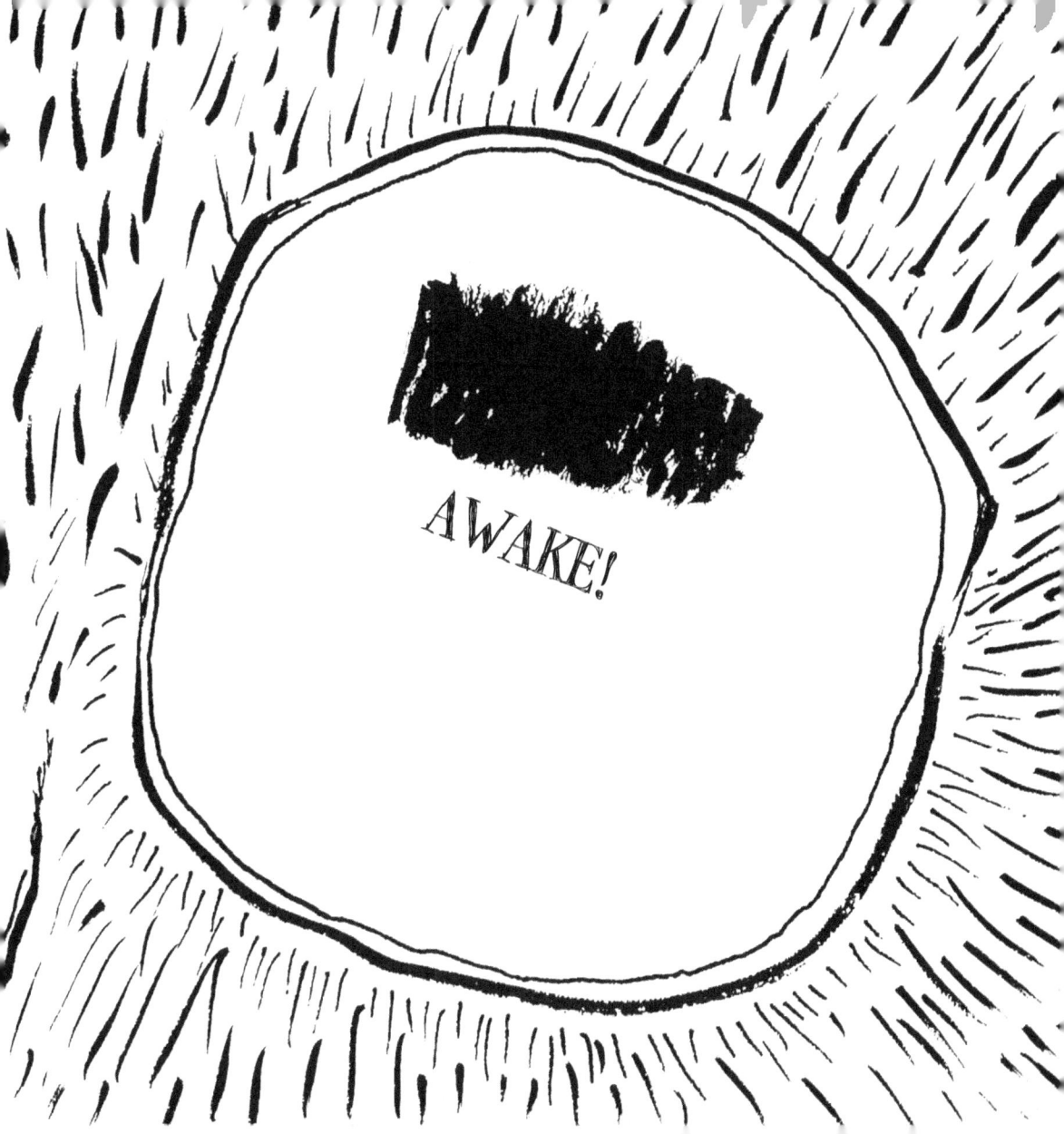

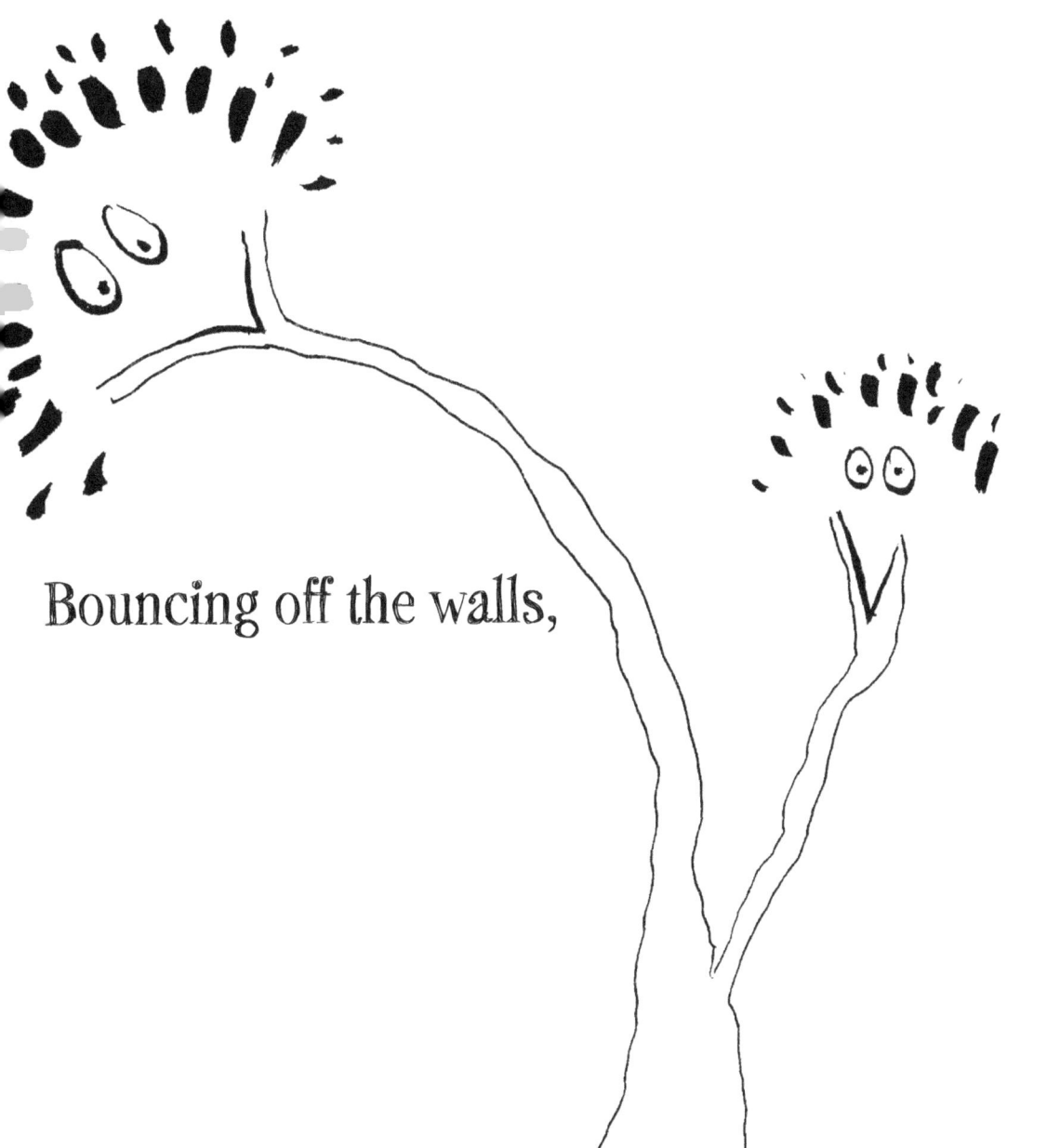

Uh Oh,

Oh no—

Fear....

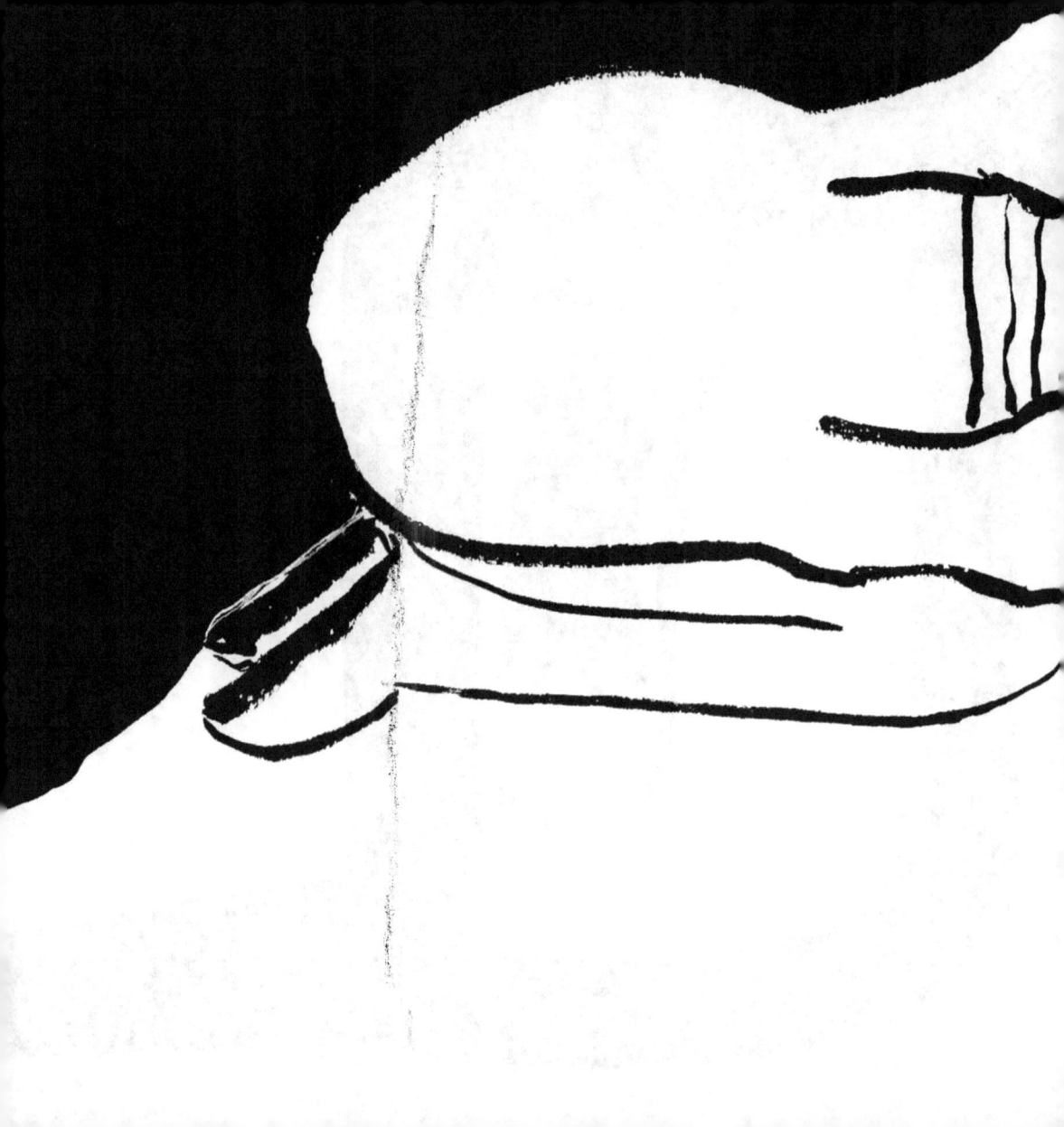

I'll hide under a rock...

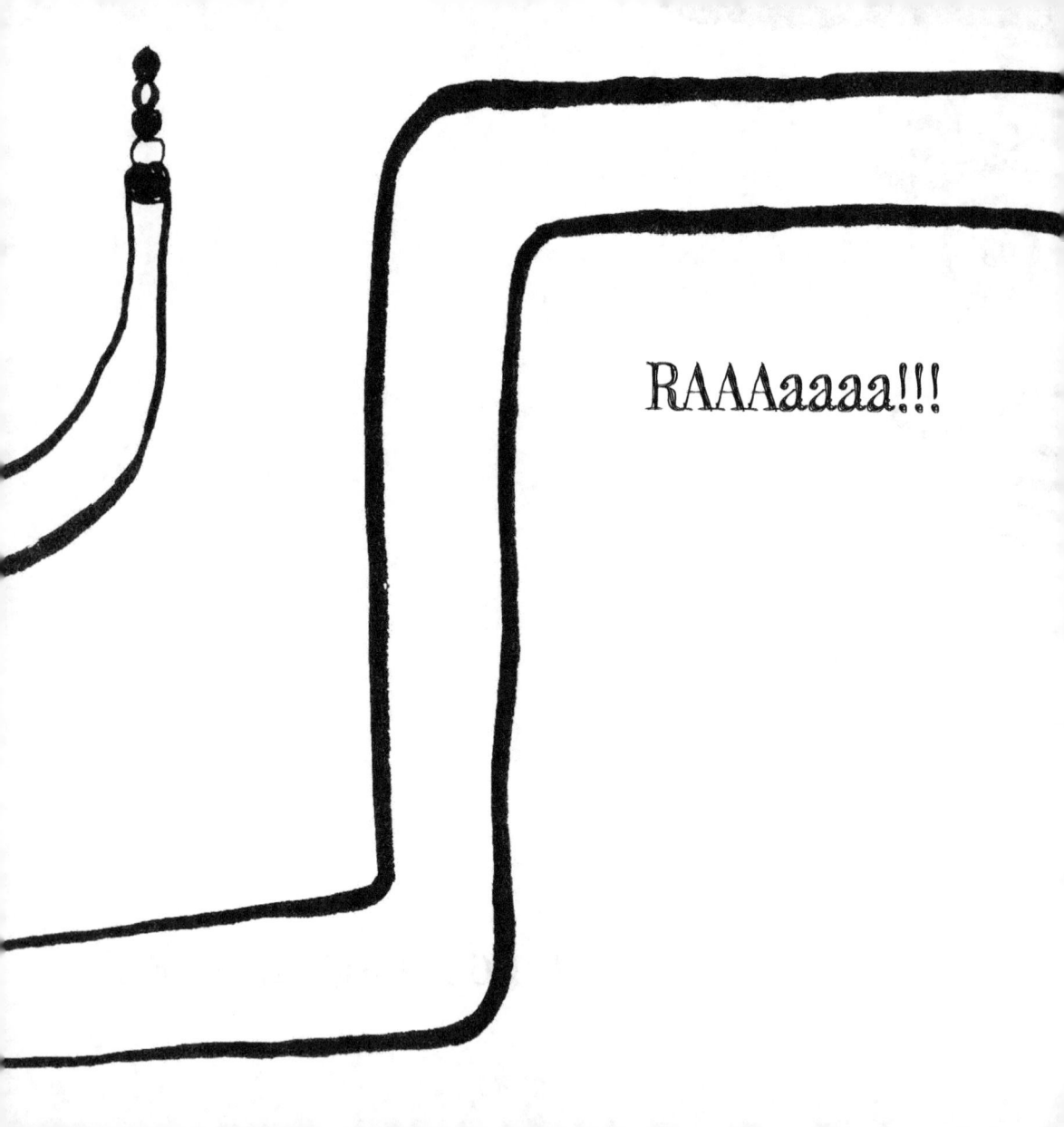

A moment to shift my perception,

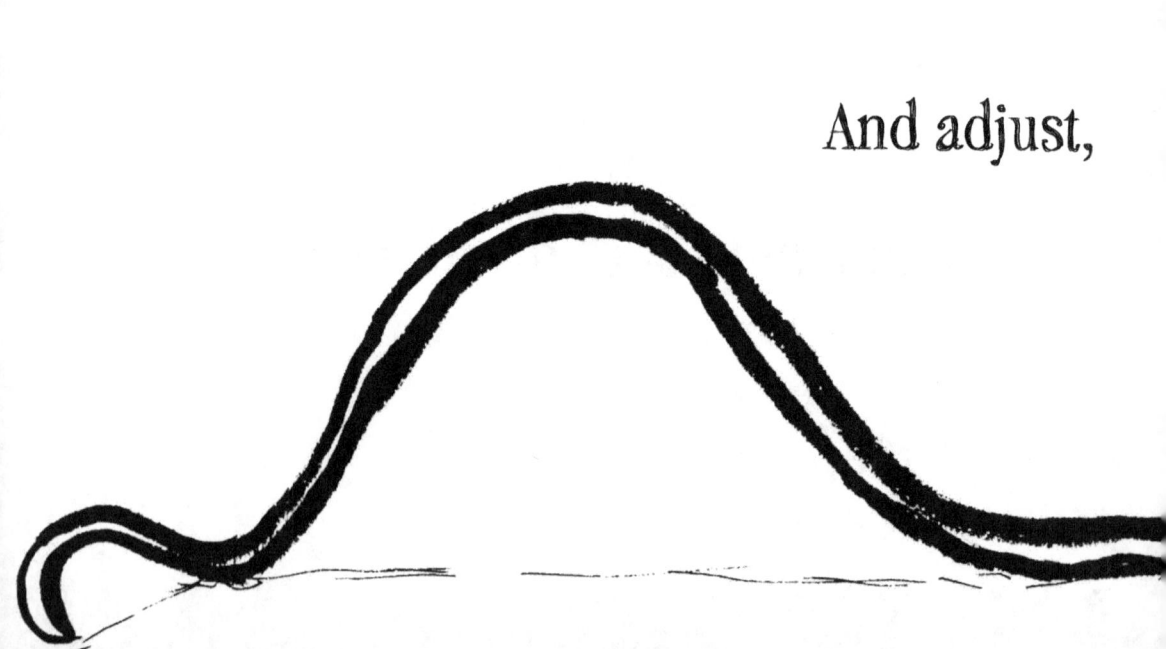
And adjust,

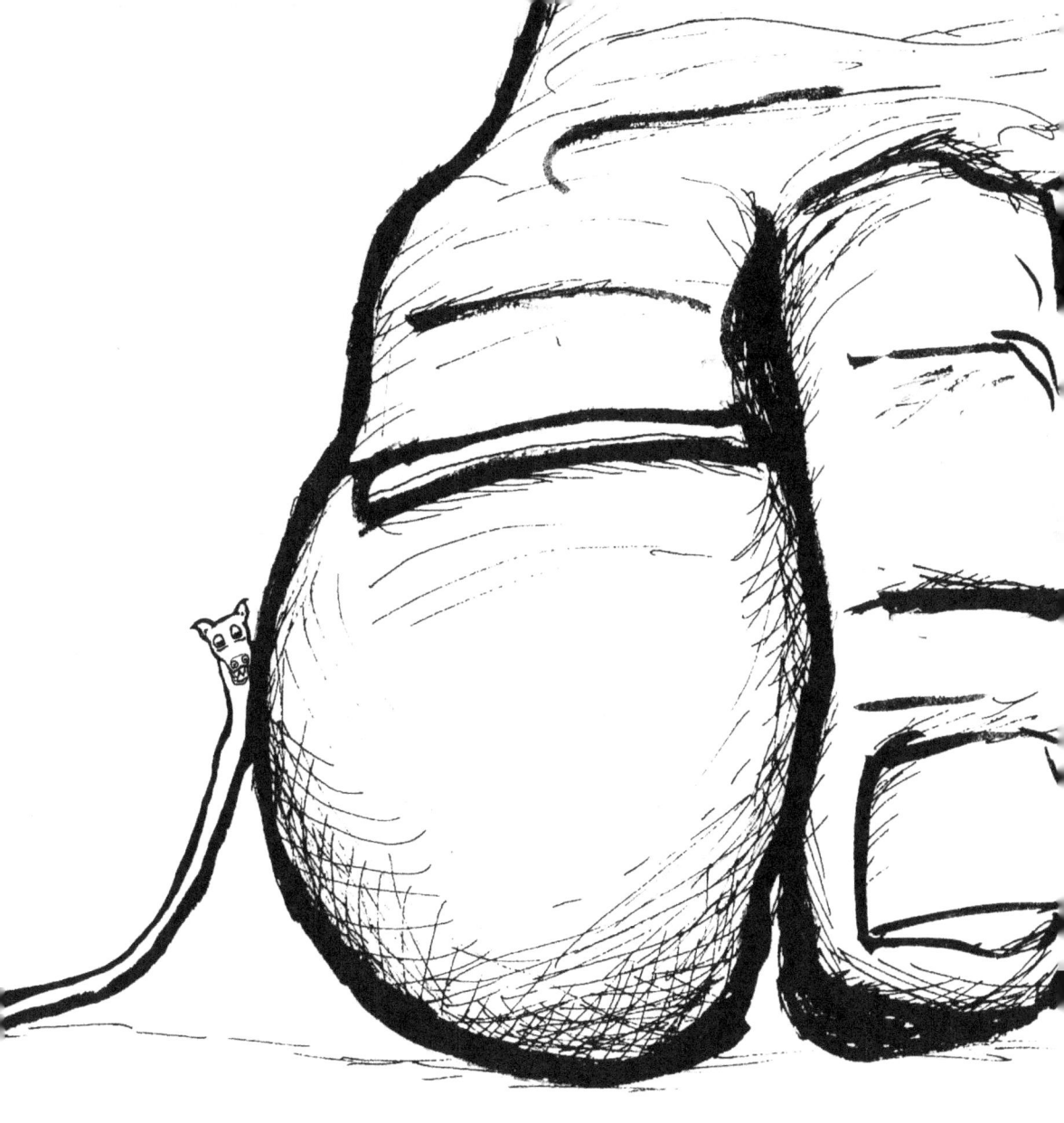

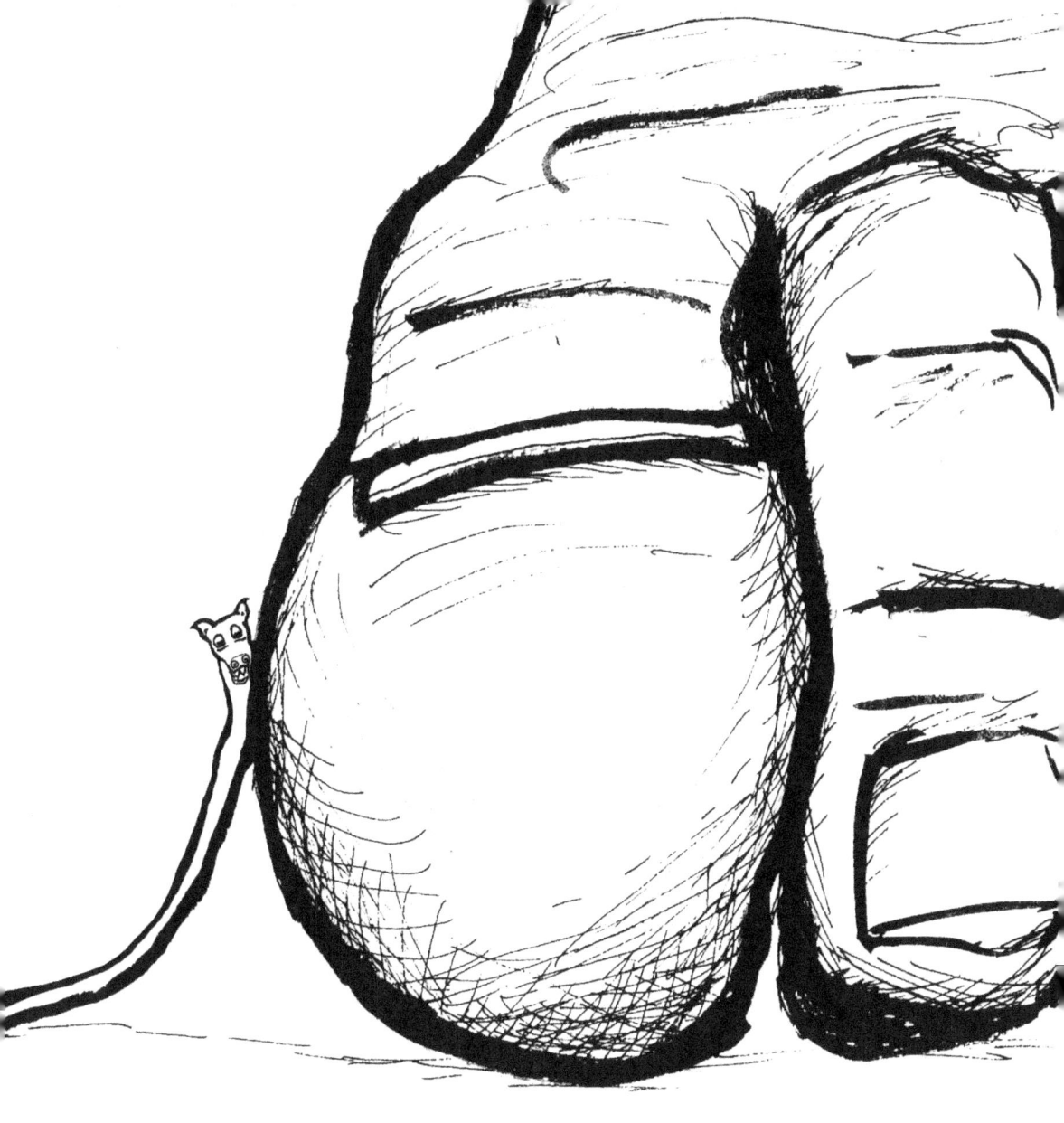

Semi-relaxed,

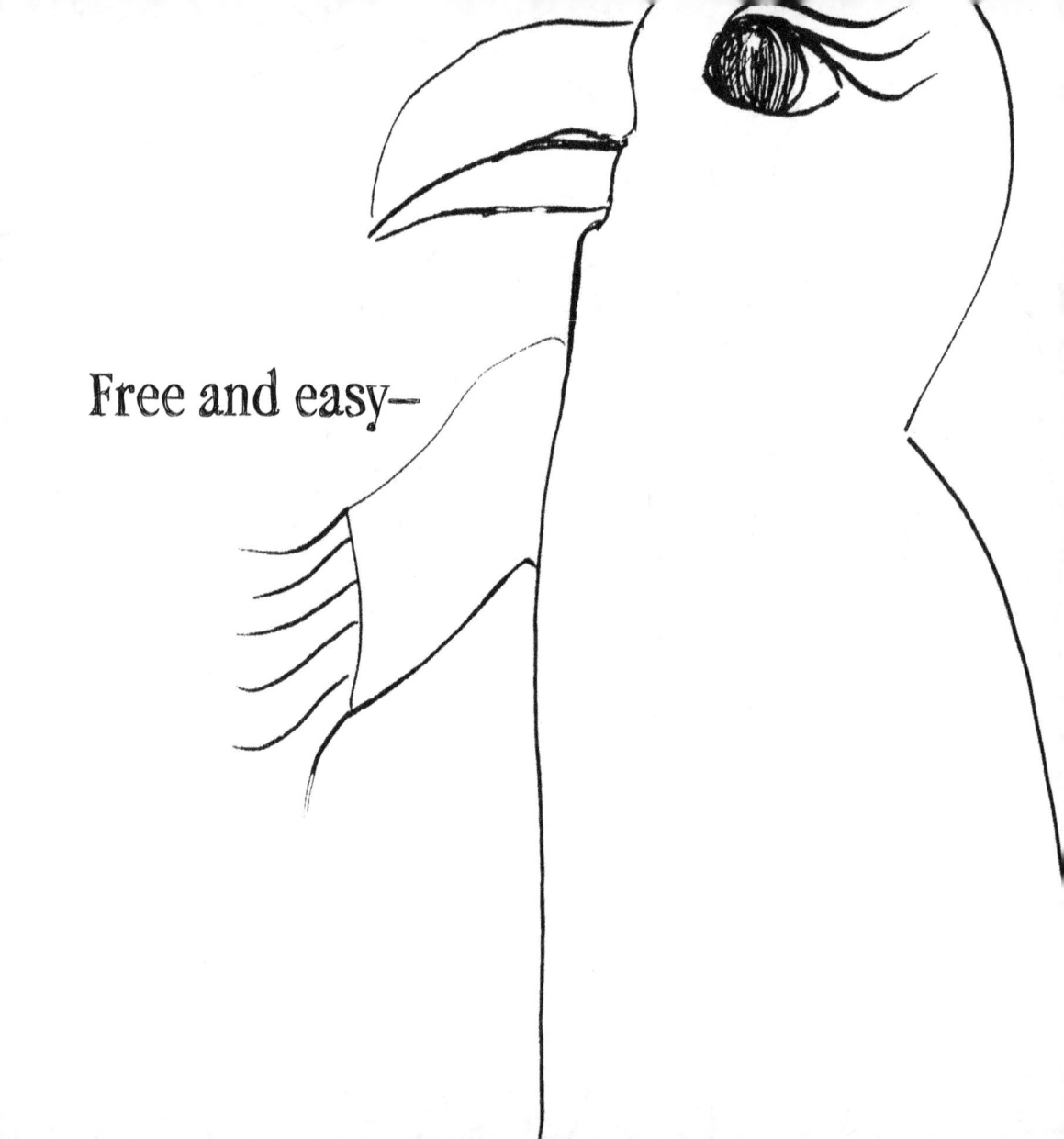

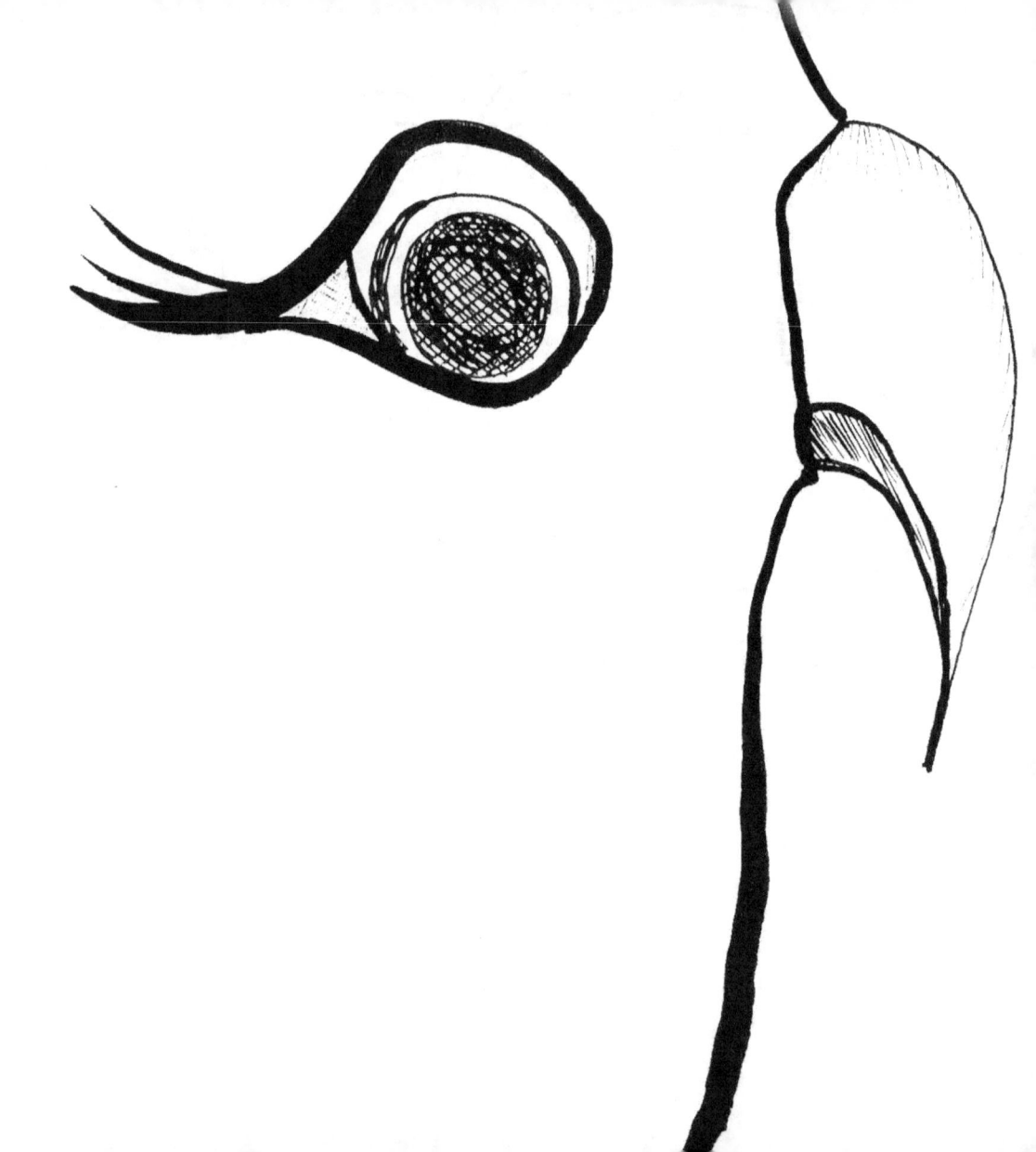

—Easy as.

Do you know who you are?

You are now—

You are this moment.

Lucky there is only one you,

and it's your choice

which mood you are.

Just Love—

and your family will know you.

So play any face you feel like.

www.ingramcontent.com/pod-product-compliance
Lightning Source LLC
Chambersburg PA
CBHW081402080526
44588CB00016B/2569